KV-512-493

for Evelyn O'Neill

Say What You Mean in English Book Two

John Andrews

Illustrated by Peter Joyce

Nelson

Thomas Nelson and Sons Ltd
Lincoln Way Windmill Road
Sunbury-on-Thames Middlesex TW16 7HP

P.O. Box 73146 Nairobi Kenya

8A Caledonia Avenue Kingston 5 Jamaica

Thomas Nelson (Australia) Ltd
19–39 Jeffcott Street West Melbourne Victoria 3003

Thomas Nelson and Sons (Canada) Ltd
81 Curlew Drive Don Mills Ontario

Thomas Nelson (Nigeria) Ltd
8 Ilupeju Bypass PMB 1303 Ikeja Lagos

© John Andrews 1977
First published 1977

ISBN 0 17 555189 8

All rights reserved. No part of this publication may
be reproduced, stored in a retrieval system, or transmitted,
in any form or by any means, electronic, mechanical,
photocopying, recording or otherwise, without the prior
permission of the publishers.

Recorded material for all books in this series is available
from the publishers.

Printed in Great Britain by
Butler & Tanner Ltd
Frome and London

Say What You Mean in English Book Two

Also available

Say What You Mean in English Book One (student's and teacher's editions)

Say What You Mean in English Workbook One

Say What You Mean in English Workbook Two

Acknowledgements

I am grateful to those teachers who have welcomed Book One as at least a step in the right direction; and in particular to those teachers overseas who have paid me the compliment of integrating Book One into their own syllabus, supplying supplementary material adapted to the local situation. I am indebted to the authors of the Oral Examinations of the Association of Recognised English Language Schools in Britain, and to the contributors to the Council of Europe's working party document on the 'Threshold Level' for modern language teaching whose requirements I have tried to keep constantly in view while preparing Book Two. My thanks are also due to Mr L. G. Alexander for the thoughts he expressed in an article published in the English Language Teaching Journal (January 1976), entitled 'Where do we go from here?'; I have attempted to follow his suggestions as far as was possible within a limited compass. Finally I wish to thank Sandra Nicholson for her help in the production of the book, and Pauline Walker for her typing.

John Andrews

Contents

Introduction

This is Book 2 in the series 'Say What You Mean in English', and is preceded by Book 1 and Workbook 1. It follows the same format as Book 1, and so teachers and students familiar with that book should find it easy to work from.

It contains what is essentially oral material, and aims to increase comprehension and promote fluency in using English socially.

The material has been selected and arranged on the basis of its communicative value, and this at all times takes priority over any grammatical ordering of structures.

There are 25 units, grouped into five broad notional categories, each unit dealing with a particular language function.

The learner is called upon to perform relatively easy tasks: to listen; to repeat what he hears; to look at the formation of the utterances he is making; and to ask and answer questions orally.

The utterances are quite short, and therefore — it is hoped — easily memorable. Care has been taken to include only utterances of high frequency in present-day spoken communication.

There is recorded material to accompany the book, and the sections recorded are marked ▶ in the text.

Teacher's Notes to accompany this book are available as a separate booklet, containing notes on each unit giving hints on preparation, presentation and follow-up. There is also a Workbook providing written exercises for reinforcement.

John Andrews   Norwood,
                                               London SE25

Plan of the units

Quick-reference grammatical guide

Present continuous   3, 8, 16   Reported Speech   5, 21
Simple Past   2, 10, 17   Passive   4, 12, 20
Past Cont. v. S. Past   3   Gerund   4, 16, 21, 22, 23, 25
Present Perfect   2, 3, 6, 15, 19   Future & Fut. Continuous   3

See the INDEX (at back of book) for occurrence of new vocabulary not presented in Book 1.

Unit	Function	Structures presented
1	Factual information	Where's the . . . ? There's one . . . How do I get there? What time's the . . . ? Which . . . ? How much is . . . ? I'll take it. How far is it? How long does it take?
2	Narration	When did you . . . ? I left/took/phoned, etc. What time did he . . . ? How did he . . . ? Did he . . . ? Have you ever been . . . ? How long were you there? Where did you stay? What did you see?
3	Explanation	What are you doing? We're . . . ing Why are you . . . ing? Because . . . Where were you? While she was . . . ing it happened. She was . . . ing when it happened. Have you finished . . . ? When do you think it'll be ready? Will you be able to . . . ? I'll be . . . ing.

4	Instructions	Do it. It must/should be done. First, you have to . . . , then . . . You may do it. It may be done. It needs no . . . ing. . . . ing must be avoided.
5	Reporting what you hear	He wants to know where . . . He wonders whether . . . He says he . . . He asks her to . . . He asked me where . . . He wanted to know whether . . . He said he . . . He asked me to . . . He told me he had . . . He told them to . . .
6	Introductions	May I introduce . . . ? How d'you do? I'd like you to meet . . . Pleased to meet you. I don't think you've met . . .
7	Invitations	Won't you join us? Oh, come on! Why don't you . . . ? I'd love to. We'd be glad if you could come. I'm afraid I can't manage . . .
8	Polite conversation	May I join you? You're not English, are you? Which part of . . . are you from? What are you doing . . . ? Have you been here long? How long are you staying? Do you live near here? Excuse me – do you mind if . . . ? Would you like to . . . ?
9	Offering	Shall I . . . ? Can I help you? Would you like me to . . . ? Is there anything you would like me to . . . ?

10	Thanking and taking leave	Thank you for . . .
		I really enjoyed it.
		Actually, we'll have to be thinking of going.
		I'm afraid we'll have to.
		It was very kind of you to . . .
		Thank you once again for . . .

11	Agreement and disagreement	I prefer . . .
		So do I/Neither did I.
		I think it's . . .
		I disagree.
		All right, I agree with you about . . .
		I'm afraid I can't agree.
		What do you object to?
		I think it will do.
		No, I don't think it will.
		Perhaps you're right.
		I'm not sure I agree with you.

12	Satisfaction and dissatisfaction	Is it what you wanted?
		Are they all right?
		Yes, it's fine.
		They'll do very nicely.
		They're perfectly all right.
		Shall I get it done?
		I'm not too happy about it.
		It's not at all what I wanted.
		It'll have to be done again.
		I can't possibly accept it.

13	Certainty and doubt	Are you sure?
		Yes, positive.
		I'm not sure.
		I couldn't say.
		I wonder if she'd like to . . . ?
		I doubt it.
		Surely you're not going to . . . ?
		I certainly am!
		Do you think he'll be . . . ?
		He might.

14	Advice	You should/shouldn't do it.
		You ought to/ought not to . . .
		I wouldn't . . . if I were you.
		Why don't you . . . ?

20	Disappointment and disgust	I'm disappointed in . . . I don't think much of . . . I suppose I'll just have to put up with it. What a mess! Just look at . . . ! It's disgraceful! They ought to be ashamed of themselves. It ought not to be allowed. They should be made to . . . It's disgraceful/offensive/dreadful. I can't bear to . . . I don't think I can stand it.
21	Commands	Do this. Stop doing that. Don't . . . , just . . . You are to/are not to . . . He told them to/not to . . . Don't . . . , or I'll . . . Don't . . . until you have . . .
22	Requests	Could you just . . . for me? Just . . . , will you? Will you . . . , please? Would you mind . . . ing? Not at all. I wonder if I could trouble you to . . . Would you be so kind as to . . .
23	Wishes	I wish I had . . ./I knew . . . I wish you would . . . If only I had . . . If only he would . . . I'd like it done. It needs doing. I don't suppose you could . . . ? I'd rather you did it.
24	Obligation	I have to . . . I must . . . You needn't . . . She doesn't have to . . . You mustn't . . .

You're not allowed to . . .
It's not allowed.
I had to/didn't have to . . .
You needn't have done it.
I'll have to/I won't have to . . .

---

25   Restraining

You shouldn't really be . . . ing.
You shouldn't really do it.
Don't keep . . . ing!
You're not supposed to . . .
You're not meant to . . .
I'd rather you didn't . . .

Unit 1
Factual information

Excuse me —
where's the nearest bank?

What time's the next train to
Norbury?

How much is this one?

How far is it to Brighton?

▶ Listen to this:

> *Woman:* Excuse me —
>   where's the nearest bank?
>   *Man:* There's one opposite the station.
> *Woman:* How do I get there, please?
>   *Man:* You go to the end of the square,
>   cross the main road,
>   turn left,
>   right at the lights,
>   and take the first on the left.
> *Woman:* Thanks very much.

▶ Now say this (listen and repeat):

> There's a bank opposite the station.
> Go to the end of the square,
> cross the main road,
> turn left,
> right at the lights,
> and take the first on the left.

Look at this:

Where's the nearest	bank? post office? bus-stop?	There's one	opposite the station. in the next street. at the crossroads.

How do I get there?	Go to the main road, turn right, cross the road, left at the church, and take the second turning on the right.

▶ Listen to this:

> *Woman:* What time's the next train to Norbury?
>   *Man:* Nine thirty-seven (9.37).
> *Woman:* Which platform?
>   *Man:* Platform ten.
> *Woman:* Thanks a lot.

▶ Now say this (listen and repeat):

> The next train to Norbury's at 9.37.
> It leaves from Platform 10.

▶ Listen to this:

> *Man:* How much is this one?
> *Woman:* Seventy-five pence (75p).
> *Man:* Is there a smaller size?
> *Woman:* Yes, there's this one.
> *Man:* How much is that?
> *Woman:* Forty-seven.
> *Man:* Right. I'll take the smaller one.
> Thanks.

▶ Now say this (listen and repeat):

This one's 75p.
The smaller one's 47.
I'll take the smaller one.

Look at this:

How much is	this? that? this one? that one? the smaller one? the larger one?	It's This one's That one's	45p. 75p. £1.20.

Read aloud these train times:

6.50	11.37	2.22	4.40
7.12	12.59	3.30	8.11
9.25	1.48	4.14	9.04

▶ Listen to this:

> *Man:* How far is it to Brighton?
> *Woman:* 54 miles.
> *Man:* How many kilometres is that?
> *Woman:* About 90.
> *Man:* How long does it take to get there?
> *Woman:* It's an hour by train,
> and about two hours by car.

▶ Now say this (listen and repeat):

It's 54 miles to Brighton.
That's about 90 kilometres.
It takes an hour by train,
and about two hours by car.

Ask and answer questions with your neighbour, like these:

Where's the nearest . . . ?
How do I get there?
How far is it?
How long does it take?

How much is this one?
Is there a larger size?
How much is that?

What time's the next bus to . . . ?
What time's the next train to . . . ?
Which platform?

Unit 2
Narration

His plane landed at 5.15.

He took a taxi from the city terminal.

She didn't go up the Empire State Building . . .

. . . but she saw it from the air.

▶ Listen to this:

> *Teacher:* When did you arrive in England?
> *Student:* Last Saturday.
> *Teacher:* Tell me about your journey.
> *Student:* I left home after lunch.
> My father drove me to the airport.
> My plane landed at Heathrow at 5.15.
> I took the airport bus to the city terminal.
> Then I phoned my English family.
> I took a taxi to their address,
> and I got there at about 7.30.

▶ Now say this (listen and repeat):

> He arrived in England last Saturday.
> He left home after lunch.
> His father drove him to the airport.
> His plane landed at Heathrow at 5.15.
> He took the airport bus to the city terminal.
> Then he phoned his English family.
> He took a taxi to their address,
> and he got there at about 7.30.

Answer these questions:

> When did he arrive in England?
> What time did he leave home?
> How did he get to the airport?
> What time did his plane land?
> How did he get to the city terminal?
> What did he do next?
> Then what did he do?
> What time did he get there?

Look at this:

How did you get	to the airport? to the city terminal? to your English family?	My father drove me. I took the airport bus. I took a taxi.

and this:

Did he arrive on Sunday?	No, he didn't. He arrived on Saturday.

Now answer these questions *in the same way*:

> Did he leave home before lunch?
> Did he take a taxi from his home to the airport?
> Did he go by train to the city terminal?
> Did he go by bus to his English family?
> Did he get there at 10 o'clock?

▶ Listen to this:

> *Man:* Have you ever been to New York?
> *Woman:* Yes, I was there last year.
> *Man:* How long were you there?
> *Woman:* Only for two days.
> *Man:* Where did you stay?
> *Woman:* In a small hotel near Central Park.
> *Man:* What did you see while you were there?
> *Woman:* Oh, most of the sights —
> Broadway, Fifth Avenue . . .
> What I liked best was the Museum of Modern Art.
> *Man:* Did you go up the Empire State Building?
> *Woman:* No, I didn't; but I saw it from the air.
> I took a helicopter flight over Manhattan.
> It was fantastic.

▶ Now say this (listen and repeat):

> She went to New York last year.
> She was only there for two days.
> She stayed in a small hotel near Central Park.
> She saw most of the sights.
> What she liked best was the Museum of Modern Art.
> She didn't go up the Empire State Building;
> but she saw it from the air.
> She took a helicopter flight.

Answer these questions:

> When was she in New York?
> How long did she stay?
> Where did she stay?
> What did she see?
> What did she like best?
> Did she go up the Empire State Building?

Look at this:

	No, I haven't. Yes, I have. I've been there twice. I was there last year. I only stayed for two days, but I saw most of the sights.
Have you ever been there?	

Now answer these questions about yourself:

Tell me the most interesting city you have ever visited.
When were you there?
How long did you stay?
Where did you stay?
What did you see?
What did you like best?
What didn't you like?
Where did you go when you left?

Unit 3
Explanation

Why are you waiting outside? Because the door's locked.

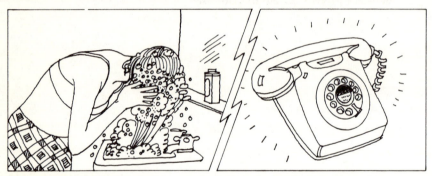

She was washing her hair . . . when the phone rang.

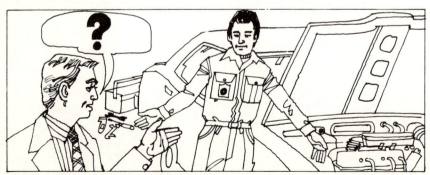

Have you finished the work on my car?
I'm afraid not. We haven't got the parts yet.

▶ Listen to this:

> *Man:* What are you doing here?
> *Boy:* We're waiting for the meeting to start.
> *Man:* Why are you waiting outside?
> *Boy:* Because the door's locked and we haven't got the key.
> *Man:* Is anyone doing anything about it?
> *Boy:* Yes, Tom's trying to get the key. He's just phoning.

▶ Now say this (listen and repeat):

> They're waiting for the meeting to start.
> The door's locked,
> and they haven't got the key,
> so they're waiting outside.
> Tom's doing something about it.
> He's trying to get the key.
> He's just phoning.

Look at this:

What	are you	doing?	We're waiting.
	is Tom		He's phoning.

Why are you waiting outside?	Because	the door's locked.
		we haven't got the key.

Answer these questions:

> What are the boys doing?
> Why are they waiting outside?
> Is anyone doing anything about it?
> What's he doing now?

▶ Listen to this:

> *Boy:* Where were you last night?
>   I tried to ring you.
> *Girl:* I was in all evening.
>   The phone rang while I was washing my hair.
>   I couldn't answer it. I'm sorry.
> *Boy:* That's all right.
>   I thought perhaps you were working late.

▶ Now say this (listen and repeat):

> He tried to ring her last night.
> The phone rang while she was washing her hair.
> She was washing her hair when the phone rang,
> so she couldn't answer it.
> He thought she was working late,
> but she wasn't.

Look at this:

> WHILE she WAS WASHING her hair, the phone RANG.

> She WAS WASHING her hair WHEN the phone RANG.

Answer these questions:

> Was she out last night?
> What was she doing when the phone rang?
> Could she answer it?
> What did he think she was doing?

▶ Listen to this:

> *1st man:* Have you finished the work on my car?
> *2nd man:* I'm afraid not.
> We haven't got the parts yet.
> *1st man:* Oh, that's a nuisance.
> When do you think it'll be ready?
> *2nd man:* Well . . . we're getting the parts in the morning.
> You'll be able to collect the car tomorrow evening.

▶ Now say this (listen and repeat):

> They haven't finished the work on his car.
> They haven't got the parts yet.
> They're getting them in the morning.
> He'll be able to collect the car tomorrow evening.

▶ Now *you* say what the second man says.
   Listen, and then answer:
      Have you finished the work on my car?
      . . . .
      . . . .
      Oh, that's a nuisance.
      When do you think it'll be ready?
      . . . .
      . . . .

▶ Listen to this:

      Woman: Will you be able to come to the party on Friday?
         Man: I'm afraid not.
                I'll be travelling back from Birmingham.
      Woman: Oh, what a pity.
                Will you be able to come round for a drink one evening
                next week?
         Man: I'm awfully sorry,
                I'll be working late every evening next week.

▶ Now say this (listen and repeat):

      He won't be able to go to the party.
      He'll be travelling back from Birmingham.
      He won't be able to go round for a drink.
      He'll be working late.

Look at this:

What ARE you doing?	→	I'm waiting.
What WERE you doing?	→	I was washing my hair.
What WILL you BE doing?	→	I'll be working late.

Unit 4
Instructions

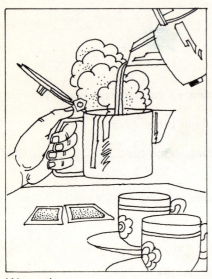

Warm the pot.

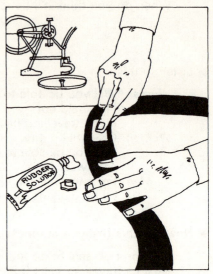

Apply the patch with firm pressure.

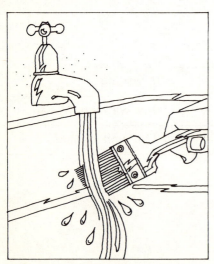

Simply wash the brush under the tap.

Stir constantly.

Read these instructions for making tea:

1. Boil some water in a kettle.
2. Take the teapot to the kettle.
3. Warm the pot by pouring in a little boiling water, and then empty it out.
4. Drop in two tea-bags (or: one per person).
5. Pour on boiling water.
6. Allow to stand for 2–3 minutes, then pour.

▶ Now say this (listen and repeat):

Some water must be boiled in a kettle.
The teapot should be taken to the kettle.
The pot should be warmed by pouring in a little boiling water.
This water must be emptied out.
Two tea-bags should be dropped in.
Boiling water should be poured on.
The tea must be allowed to stand for two to three minutes, and should then be poured.

Look at this:

You MUST BOIL it.	→	It MUST BE BOILED.
You SHOULD TAKE it.	→	It SHOULD BE TAKEN.
You SHOULD DROP them in.	→	They SHOULD BE DROPPED in.
You MUST ALLOW it to stand.	→	It MUST BE ALLOWED to stand.

Now, tell your friend how to make tea.
Begin like this:

First, you . . . .
Then you . . . .
Next you . . . .
And then you . . . .

Read these instructions for mending a puncture in the inner tube of a bicycle tyre:

1. Thoroughly clean surface of tube around puncture.
2. Apply solution to the tube and allow to become tacky.
3. Tear off protective backing from patch and apply patch with firm pressure, particularly at edges.
4. Dust the repair to prevent adhesion to outer cover.

▶ Now say this (listen and repeat):

> The surface must be thoroughly cleaned.
> The solution must be allowed to become tacky.
> The backing should be torn off.
> The patch should be applied with firm pressure.

Now, tell your friend how to mend a puncture.
He (or she) asks: 'What do I have to do?' and you reply:

> First, you have to . . . .
> Then, you have to . . . .
> Next you have to . . . .
> And then you have to . . . .
> Don't forget to . . . .

Read these instructions for using BROLAC VINYL PAINT:

> Make sure the surface is sound, clean, dry and free from grease.
> Brolac Vinyl may be applied with brush or roller. It is supplied
> ready for use, and needs no stirring. For best results apply liberally
> and evenly with a generously loaded brush. Finish off with light
> vertical strokes, and avoid rebrushing wet areas. A second coat
> may be applied 3–4 hours after application of the first coat.
> To clean, simply wash the brush under the tap.

▶ Now say this (listen and repeat):

> You may apply it with brush or roller.
> It needs no stirring.
> You should apply it liberally and evenly.
> You should finish off with light vertical strokes.
> Re-brushing wet areas must be avoided.
> You may apply a second coat three to four hours after the first
> coat.

Answer these questions about using BROLAC VINYL PAINT:

> What must the surface be like?
> What can you apply the paint with?
> Does it need stirring?
> How should you finish off?
> What must you avoid doing?
> How soon can you apply a second coat?

Look at this:

The paint	may should must	be applied liberally.

Read these instructions for making CAMPBELL'S CONDENSED SOUP:

Makes double the quantity. Here's how:
Empty the soup into a saucepan and stir. Add one full can of water, a little at a time, stirring constantly. Heat to boiling, stirring occasionally.

▶ Now say this (listen and repeat):

The soup should be emptied into a saucepan and stirred.
A full can of water should be added, a little at a time.
The soup should be heated to boiling, and should be stirred occasionally.

Tell your friend how to make the soup.
Begin with:

First you . . . .
Then you . . . .

Unit 5
Reporting what you hear

▶ Listen to this:

> *(Man):* 'Where's my watch?'
> 'Have you seen it?'
> 'I can't find it.'
> 'I really need it.'
> 'I haven't got much time.'
> 'I'll be late.'
> 'Will you help me look for it?'

▶ Now say this (listen and repeat):

> He wants to know where his watch is.
> He wonders whether she has seen it.
> He says he can't find it.
> He says he really needs it.
> He says he hasn't got much time.
> He says he'll be late.
> He asks her to help him look for it.

▶ Listen to this:

> *(Woman):* Yesterday he asked me where his watch was.
> He wanted to know whether I had seen it.
> He said he couldn't find it.
> He said he really needed it.
> He said he hadn't got much time.
> He said he'd be late.
> He asked me to help him look for it.

▶ Now say this (listen and repeat):

> He asked her where his watch was.
> He wanted to know whether she had seen it.
> He said he couldn't find it.
> He said he needed it.
> He said he hadn't got much time.
> He said he'd be late.
> He asked her to help him look for it.

Look at this:

'Where's my watch?'	A He wants to know where his watch is.
	B He asked me where his watch was.
'Have you seen it?'	A He wonders whether she has seen it.
	B He wanted to know whether she had seen it.
'I can't find it.'	A He says he can't find it.
	B He said he couldn't find it.
'I'll be late.'	A He says he'll be late. (he'll = he will)
	B He said he'd be late. (he'd = he would)

Now report these sentences, using 'Type A' reports (see the table).

'Where's my pen?'
'Have you borrowed it?'
'I can't see it anywhere.'
'I haven't got another one.'
'Can you lend me one?'

Now report the same sentences, using 'Type B' reports (see the table).

▶ Listen to this:

(Man): 'I've parked my car at the station.'
'I've lost my car keys.'
'My wife has the spare keys,
so I'll have to go home by taxi.'

▶ Now say this (listen and repeat):

He told me he had parked his car at the station,
and that he had lost his car keys.

He said his wife had the spare keys,
so he'd have to go home by taxi.

Look at this:

| He told me He said | he had done it. |

▶ Listen to this:

> *Man:* 'Help me with the luggage, will you?'
> *Woman:* 'Mind your head!'
> *Man:* 'Go away and don't come back!'

▶ Now say this (listen and repeat):

> He asked her to help him with the luggage.
> She warned him to mind his head.
> He told them to go away and not to come back.

Report these sentences in the same way:

> *(Woman):* 'Be quiet!'
> *(Man):* 'Make me a cup of coffee, will you?'
> *(Woman):* 'Put it down and don't touch it again!'
> *(Man):* 'Mind the step!'
> *(Woman):* 'Please speak more slowly.'
> *(Woman):* 'Please don't speak so fast.'

▶ Listen to this:

> *(Man):* 'I found this purse in the street outside my house.'
> He said he had found the purse in the street outside
> his house.
> *(Woman):* 'I saw him yesterday.'
> She said she had seen him the day before.

▶ Now say this (listen and repeat):

> He said he had found the purse
> in the street outside his house.
>
> She said she had seen him the day before.

Look at this:

'I need it.'	→	He said he needed it.
'I can't find it.'	→	He said he couldn't find it.
'I'll be late.'	→	He said he'd be late.
'I've lost it.'	→	He said he had lost it.
'I found it in the street.'	→	He said he had found it in the street.
'Where is it?'	→	He asked where it was.
'Help me, will you?'	→	He asked her to help him.
'Go away!'	→	She told them to go away.
'Mind your head!'	→	She warned him to mind his head.

Unit 6
Introductions

May I introduce Mr Thorn?

How d'you do?

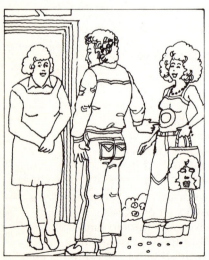

I'd like you to meet Denise.

Tom, this is Susi.

▶ Listen to this:

> Susi: Mr Coleman, may I introduce Mr Thorn?
> He's my English teacher.
> Coleman: How d'you do?
> Thorn: How d'you do?
> Coleman: Susi's told us quite a lot about you.
> Thorn: Oh, dear — nothing too terrible, I hope?
> Coleman: No, not at all. She's very happy about things.

▶ Now say this (listen and repeat):

> May I introduce Mr Thorn?
> He's my English teacher.
> How d'you do?
> How d'you do?
> Susi's told us about you.
> Oh, dear — nothing terrible, I hope?
> Not at all. She's very happy.

▶ Listen to this:

> Mario: Mrs Wilkins, I'd like you to meet Denise.
> She's at school with me.
> Mrs W: Hallo, Denise.
> Pleased to meet you.
> Won't you come in?
> Denise: Thank you.
> Mrs W: How long have you been over here?
> Denise: Not very long.
> I started school last week.

▶ Now say this (listen and repeat):

> I'd like you to meet Denise.
> She's at school with me.
> Hallo, Denise.
> Pleased to meet you.
> Won't you come in?
> Thanks.
> How long have you been over here?
> Not very long.
> I started school last week.

Read the conversations again, and answer these questions:

Who's Mr Thorn?
Who's Susi?
Is she happy about things?

Who's Denise?
What's she doing in England?
When did she start school?

Look at this:

May I introduce I'd like you to meet	Mr Thorn. Denise.	How d'you do? Pleased to meet you.

▶ Listen to this:

   John: Hi, Susi!
         How are you?
   Susi: Fine, thanks. And you?
   John: Yes, I'm all right.
         Susi – I don't think you've met Tom, have you?
         Tom, this is Susi.
   Tom: Hallo, Susi.
         Actually, we've already met.
   John: Have you?
   Susi: Yes – we're in the same class!
   John: Really? I didn't know.

▶ Now say this (listen and repeat):

Hi, Susi. How are you?
Fine, thanks. And you?
Yes, I'm all right.
I don't think you've met Tom, have you?
Actually, we've already met.
We're in the same class.
Really? I didn't know.

Look at this:

May I introduce . . .
I'd like you to meet . . .
I don't think you've met . . .
This is . . .

Hallo, . . .
Pleased to meet you.
How d'you do?
We've already met.

Now practise some introductions:

Introduce your neighbour to another student;
        your neighbour to your teacher;
        your teacher to 'a new student'.

Now play these roles, and make the introductions:

Introduce a friend to your landlady;
        a boyfriend (or girlfriend) to your mother;
        a new employee to the boss;
        a new employee to your colleagues;
        your sister to your teacher.

Unit 7
Invitations

We're just going for a drink.
Won't you join us?

Why don't you come round
for a meal?
I'd love to.

We'd be glad if you could
come.
I'm afraid I can't manage it.

▶ Listen to this:

> *Man:* Listen — we're just going round the corner for a drink. Won't you join us?
> *Woman:* Well — I'd like to, but I'm not sure I have time.
> *Man:* Oh, come on! Just a quick one!
> *Woman:* All right, just a quick one.

▶ Now say this (listen and repeat):

> They're just going for a drink.
> They want her to join them.
> She'd like to,
> but she's not sure she has time.
> She says she'll go,
> just for a quick one.

▶ Listen to this:

> *Woman:* Why don't you come round for a meal one evening next week?
> *Man:* I'd love to.
> *Woman:* Which day would suit you?
> *Man:* Any day except Wednesday.
> *Woman:* How about Friday?
> *Man:* Yes, Friday would be fine. What time shall I come?
> *Woman:* Oh, about 6.30 — will that be all right?
> *Man:* Yes, of course. Thank you very much.
> *Woman:* See you on Friday, then.

▶ Now say this (listen and repeat):

> She wants him to go round for a meal.
> He says he'd love to.
> She asks which day would suit him.
> She suggests Friday, and he agrees.
> He asks what time he should come.
> She suggests 6.30, and he agrees.

Look at this:

Won't you Why don't you	join us? come round for a meal?	I'd like to. I'd love to.

Now practise inviting someone:

Invite your neighbour to join you and your friends for a drink.
Use these words:

1. *You say* −	*Your neighbour says* −
. . . round the corner for a drink	. . . not sure . . . time.
. . . join us?	
. . . a quick one.	All right . . .

2. *You say* −	*Your neighbour says* −
. . . a meal one evening next week?	Yes, . . .
Which evening . . . ?	Any . . . except . . .
How about . . . ?	Yes, . . .
	What time . . . ?
. . . 7.30.	. . . fine.

Now practise these invitations in the same way:

invite your friend to join you for a cup of coffee in the snack-bar;
invite your friend to go to the cinema with you one evening next week;
invite your friend to play tennis with you.

▶ Listen to this:

Man: Look − we're having one or two people round for dinner next Tuesday. We'd be glad if you could come.
Woman: Well, that's very kind of you −
but I'm afraid I can't manage Tuesday.
I've got something else on.
Man: Oh, what a pity. Some other time, perhaps?
Woman: Yes, I'd love to come some other time, if it can be arranged.
Man: I'll have a word with Jane and let you know.
Woman: Thanks very much.

▶ Now say this (listen and repeat):

He'd like her to go to dinner next Tuesday.
She can't manage Tuesday.
She's got something else on.
He says he'll invite her some other time.

Look at this:

Won't you join us? Why don't you come? We'd be glad if you could come.	Well, that's very kind of you, but I'm afraid I can't manage it.

Now refuse these invitations politely:

We're just going for a drink. Can you come?
We're going out for a meal tomorrow evening. Would you like to come?
I'm driving to Oxford on Saturday. Why don't you come too?
We're going out for a picnic on Sunday. We'd be glad if you could join us.

Unit 8
Polite conversation

May I join you?
Please do!

Do you live near here?
Yes — in one of those flats
over there.

Are you going far?
To York, actually.

► Listen to this:

> *1st man:* May I join you?
> *2nd man:* Please do!
> You're not English, are you?
> *1st man:* No, I'm French.
> *2nd man:* Which part of France are you from?
> *1st man:* The west coast — near Bordeaux.
> *2nd man:* What are you doing over here?
> *1st man:* I'm learning English.
> *2nd man:* Have you been here long?
> *1st man:* No, only for two weeks.
> *2nd man:* How long are you staying?
> *1st man:* Another ten weeks — three months altogether.
> *2nd man:* Oh, perhaps we'll meet again.
> Can I get you another drink?
> *1st man:* Well, that's very kind of you.
> Thank you very much.

► Now say this (listen and repeat):

> He's not English, he's French.
> He's from the west coast, near Bordeaux.
> He's learning English.
> He hasn't been here long —
> only for two weeks.
> He's staying for three months.
> Perhaps they'll meet again.

Now answer these questions about yourself:

> You're not English, are you?
> . . . .
> Which part are you from?
> . . . .
> What are you doing over here?
> . . . .
> Have you been here long?
> . . . .
> How long are you staying?
> . . . .
> Can I get you another drink?
> . . . .

Look at this:

I'm	French. from the west coast.
He's	learning English. staying for three months.

▶ Listen to this:

Woman: Lovely weather!
Man: Yes, it's really warm.
Woman: I've seen you before, haven't I?
Man: Well, you may have done.
    I've been here once or twice.
    Do you live near here?
Woman: Yes, I live in one of those flats over there.
    What about you?
Man: Oh, I'm staying with a family down near the station.
Woman: Are you on holiday?
Man: Well, partly. I'm here to improve my English.
    I'm from Greece, you see.
Woman: I didn't think you were English, but your English is very
    good.
Man: Thank you very much.

▶ Now say this (listen and repeat):

She thinks she's seen him before.
He's been here once or twice.
She lives in one of the flats over there.
He's staying with a family.
He's from Greece.
He's here to improve his English.
She didn't think he was English,
but she thinks his English is very good.

Answer these questions:

Has she seen him before?
How many times has he been there?
Where's he staying?
Is he here on holiday?
What does she think of his English?

▶ Listen to this:

> *Woman:* Excuse me — do you mind if we close the window?
> *Man:* Not at all! Let me do it.
> *Woman:* Thanks a lot.
> *Man:* Are you going far?
> *Woman:* To York, actually.
> *Man:* A beautiful city!
> Have you been there before?
> *Woman:* No, I haven't.
> *Man:* I think you'll like it.
> *Woman:* How far are you going?
> *Man:* To Edinburgh.
> I have some business to do there.
> Would you like to read this magazine?
> I've finished with it.
> *Woman:* Yes, I would.
> Thank you very much.

Look at this:

Do you mind if	I sit here? we close the window?	Not at all!

Now answer these questions:

> How far is she going?
> Has she been there before?
> What does he think of it?
> How far is he going?
> Why is he going there?
> Have you ever been to Edinburgh?

Unit 9
Offering

Shall I get you another cup of coffee?

Can I help you?

Would you like me to type it for you?

Is there anything I can do for you?

▶ Listen to this:

> *Man:* Shall I get you another cup of coffee?
> *Woman:* Yes, please. That's very kind of you.
>
> *Woman:* Shall I make some more sandwiches?
> *Man:* No, thanks. I've had plenty.

▶ Now say this (listen and repeat):

> Shall I get you another cup?
> Yes, please.
> Shall I make some more?
> No, thanks.
> He offers her another cup,
> and she accepts.
> She offers to make some more sandwiches,
> but he says he's had plenty.

Respond to these offers:

> Shall I get you another cup of coffee?
> (Say yes) . . . .
> Shall I make some more sandwiches?
> (Say no) . . . .

▶ Listen to this:

> *Man:* Can I help you?
> *Woman:* Yes, please. I'm trying to find the dictionaries.
> *Man:* They're over there, by the window.
> *Woman:* Oh, thanks very much.
>
> *Woman:* Can I help you?
> *Man:* No, thanks. I'm just looking.

▶ Now say this (listen and repeat):

> He wants to know if he can help her.
> She's looking for the dictionaries.
> He tells her where they are,
> and she thanks him.
> She offers to help him,
> but he says he's just looking.

Look at this:

Shall I get you another one?	Yes, please.	That's very kind of you.
	No, thanks.	I've had plenty.
Can I help you?	Yes, please.	I'm trying to find a dictionary.
	No, thanks.	I'm just looking.

▶ Listen to this:

Woman: Would you like me to type it for you?
Man: Yes, please – that would be a great help.
Are you sure you don't mind?
Woman: Not at all. I'll be glad to do it.
Man: Thanks very much.

Man: Would you like me to write it out again first?
Woman: No, there's no need.
Man: I could quite easily.
Woman: No, don't bother.
It's all right as it is.

▶ Now say this (listen and repeat):

Would you like me to do it?
Yes, please, that would be a great help.
Would you like me to do it again?
No, there's no need.
I could quite easily.
Are you sure you don't mind?
Not at all. I'll be glad to do it.

Look at this:

| Shall I | do it? |
| Would you like me to | |

Now, respond to these offers:

> Shall I open the window?
> Can I help you?
> Shall I explain it again?
> Would you like me to carry it for you?
> Would you like me to phone him?
> Shall I type it for you?
> Shall I write it out again first?
> Would you like me to take a photograph of you?
> Would you like me to get you anything at the shops?
> Shall I help you to get the breakfast ready?

► Listen to this:

> *Woman:* I have to get lunch.
>   *Man:* Can I help?
> *Woman:* Yes, that would be nice.
>   *Man:* Shall I cut some bread?
> *Woman:* Yes, please. That would be a help.
>   *Man:* Would you like me to wash the salad?
> *Woman:* No, there's no need, thanks.
>   I've already done it.
>   *Man:* Is there anything else you would like me to do?
> *Woman:* Well, you could lay the table.

Now imagine you and your friend are planning a party. Offer to help:

buy some wine	cut some bread
get some ice out	open the orange-juice
open some packets of nuts	put some plates out
polish the glasses	choose some records

Unit 10
Thanking and taking leave

Thank you for a lovely day.
I really enjoyed it.

More coffee?
Actually, we'll have to
be thinking of going.

Thank you for having me to
stay.
It's been a pleasure.

▶ Listen to this:

1st woman:	Thank you for a lovely day.
	I really enjoyed it.
Man:	It was nice to have you with us.
1st woman:	Thank you for the picnic, too.
	It was super.
2nd woman:	Not at all. It was a pleasure.
	Perhaps you'll come out with us again while you're here.
1st woman:	Yes, I'd love to.
	Thanks again.
	Goodbye.

▶ Now say this (listen and repeat):

Thank you for a lovely day.
Thank you for the picnic.
I really enjoyed it.
It was super.

It was nice to have you with us.
It was a pleasure.
Perhaps you'll come again.
I'd love to.

▶ Listen to this:

Man:	Well, that was a marvellous meal.
	Thank you very much.
1st woman:	Yes, it was delicious, thank you.
2nd woman:	I'm glad you liked it.
	Will you have some more coffee?
Man:	Well . . . no thanks.
	Actually, we'll have to be thinking of going.
2nd woman:	Oh, not yet, surely?
1st woman:	I'm afraid we'll have to.
	We have a long way to go.
	And it *is* 11.30.
2nd woman:	Goodness, is that the time?
Man:	Thanks again. It really was very kind of you to invite us.
2nd woman:	Not at all.
	It was a pleasure.
	You must come again.
Man:	We'd love to.

▶ Now say this (listen and repeat):

> I'm glad you liked it.
> We'll have to be thinking of going.
> Oh, not yet, surely?
> I'm afraid we'll have to.
> Thanks again.
> It was kind of you to invite us.
> It was a pleasure.
> You must come again.
> We'd love to.

Look at this:

That was	a lovely day out.	I'm glad you	liked it.
	a delicious meal.		enjoyed it.

It was	very kind	of you to invite us.
	very good	

Not at all. It was a pleasure.

▶ Listen to this:

Man: Well, here we are.
You're in plenty of time for your plane.
1st woman: Don't forget the small bag, Denise.
2nd woman: I can't believe the time has come to say goodbye.
I'm not really sure I want to leave.
1st woman: Oh, you'll be glad to get home to your family, I'm sure.
2nd woman: Yes, I suppose so.
Well, thank you both very much for having me to stay with you.
It's been like a second home for me.
1st woman: We're glad you've been happy here.
It's been a pleasure to have you.
Man: Don't forget to write to us, Denise.
2nd woman: Don't worry, I won't.
Thank you once again for all you've done for me; and for bringing me to the airport. Goodbye!

1st woman: Goodbye, Denise. We'll miss you.
Man: Goodbye. Have a good journey.

▶ Now say this (listen and repeat):

Well, here we are.
I'm not sure I want to leave.
Thank you for having me to stay.
Thank you for all you've done for me.
Thank you for bringing me to the airport.

We're glad you've been happy here.
It's been a pleasure to have you.
We'll miss you.
Have a good journey.

Now respond to these expressions of thanks:

Thank you for a lovely day. I really enjoyed it.
. . . .
That was a delicious meal; thank you very much.
. . . .
Thank you for all you've done for me.
. . . .
Thank you for bringing me to the airport.
. . . .
Thank you for having me to stay.
. . . .
Thank you for this lovely present.
. . . .
Thank you for all your help.
. . . .

What do you say?

– at the end of an evening when you've been invited, and you
  think it's time to leave;
– when someone has driven you home in his car;
– to your teacher when you are leaving school;
– to people who have you to stay for the weekend;
– at the end of a holiday, to new friends you have made.

Unit 11
Agreement and disagreement

I prefer the smaller one.
So do I.

I think Bournemouth's nicer.
I disagree. Brighton's more lively.

I'm afraid I can't agree.

I think this one will do.
No, I don't think it will.

▶ Listen to this:

> *1st man:* Which is the better of the two?
> *2nd man:* Well, I prefer the smaller one.
> *1st man:* So do I.
> Did you see the other two yesterday?
> *2nd man:* Yes. I didn't think much of them.
> *1st man:* Neither did I.

▶ Now say this (listen and repeat):

> Which do you prefer?
> The smaller one, I think.
> So do I.
> What do you think of this one?
> Not much.
> Neither do I.
> Did you like the one we saw yesterday?
> No, I didn't.
> Neither did I.
> I liked the first one we saw.
> So did I.

Look at this:

I like this one.	→	So do I.
I liked the first one.	→	So did I.
I don't like this one.	→	Neither do I.
I didn't like the first one.	→	Neither did I.

Now agree with these statements:

> I think this is a marvellous book. . . . .
> I thought the other one was better. . . . .
> I prefer the smaller one. . . . .
> I didn't think much of the film. . . . .
> I don't really like this one. . . . .

▶ Listen to this:

> *Woman:* I think Bournemouth's a much nicer town than Brighton.
> *Man:* I disagree.
> Brighton's more lively.
> And it has more interesting buildings.

Woman: Yes, but the beach is stony.
You can't beat Bournemouth for sandy beaches.
Man: Well, all right. I agree with you about that.
But I still prefer Brighton as a town.

▶ Now say this (listen and repeat):

Bournemouth's nicer.
I disagree.
Brighton's more lively.
Bournemouth beach is better.
Yes, I agree with you about that.
But I still prefer Brighton.

Answer these questions:

Which town does she prefer?
Why does he prefer Brighton?
What's the beach like at Brighton?
What are the beaches like at Bournemouth?
Do you prefer a sandy beach or a stony one?
Why?

▶ Listen to this:

Chairman: I think we should accept Smith's plan.
Director: I'm afraid I can't agree.
Chairman: What do you object to?
Director: I don't think it's very practical.
And it's too expensive.

▶ Now say this (listen and repeat):

I think we should accept it.
I'm afraid I can't agree.
What do you object to?
It's too expensive.

▶ Listen to this:

Woman: I think this one will do.
Man: No, I'm sorry.
I don't think it will.
Woman: Why? What's wrong with it?
Man: It's much too hard.
Woman: Perhaps you're right.

▶ Now say this (listen and repeat):

> This one will do, won't it?
> Yes, I think so.
> I think this one will do.
> I'm sorry, I don't think it will.
> What's wrong with it?
> It's too hard.
> Perhaps you're right.

▶ Listen to this:

> *Man:* I didn't think much of the film.
> *Woman:* Oh, I don't know. I'm not sure I agree with you.
>   It wasn't too bad.
> *Man:* I suppose not.

Now look at this:

I thought it was good.	I disagree. I'm afraid I can't agree. I'm not sure I agree with you.

Disagree with these statements. (Say *why* you disagree):

> English coffee is the best in the world.
> Sandy beaches are best for bathing.
> Camping is great fun.
> Travelling by air is horrible.
> English is an easy language to learn.

Unit 12
Satisfaction and dissatisfaction

Is it what you wanted?
Yes, it's fine.

Are they all right?
Yes, they'll do very nicely.

I'm afraid it's not at all what I
wanted.

Oh, dear! I can't possibly accept it.

▶ Listen to this:

> *1st man:* Have you read my report?
> *2nd man:* Yes, I read it last night.
> *1st man:* Is it what you wanted?
> *2nd man:* Yes, it's fine.
> *1st man:* I hope I've mentioned all the important points.
> *2nd man:* Oh, I think so. You seem to have covered everything.
> *1st man:* Shall I get copies made?
> *2nd man:* Yes, please do.

▶ Now say this (listen and repeat):

> Have you read it?
> Yes, I read it last night.
> Is it what you wanted?
> Yes, it's fine.

Answer these questions:

> Has he read the other man's report?
> When did he read it?
> Is he satisfied with it?
> What does he say about it?
> Does he want copies made?

▶ Listen to this:

> *Man:* Here are the photographs you asked me to take.
> Are they all right?
> *Woman:* Let's see.
> Oh, yes. These will do very nicely.
> *Man:* I could take some more if you like.
> *Woman:* No, there's no need.
> These are perfectly all right.

▶ Now say this (listen and repeat):

> Are they all right?
> Yes, they are.
> Will they do?
> Yes, they will.
> Shall I take some more?
> No, there's no need.
> These are all right.

Look at this:

Is it	what you wanted?	Yes,	it's	fine.
Are they	all right?		they're	perfectly all right.

Will it do?	Yes,	it will. it'll do very nicely.

Shall I	get	it typed? copies made?	Yes, please do. No, there's no need.

Answer these questions in the same way (yes or no):

Shall I get it mended?
Shall I get it cleaned?
Shall I get it copied?
Shall I get them changed?
Shall I get it photographed?

▶ Listen to this:

1st man: Here's a model of our latest design.
What do you think of it?
2nd man: Well, I'm not too happy about it.
1st man: What's wrong with it?
2nd man: Well, I'm afraid it's not at all what I wanted.
You haven't really followed my instructions.
It'll have to be done again.
1st man: Oh, dear!

▶ Now say this (listen and repeat):

What do you think of it?
I'm not too happy about it.
What's wrong with it?
It's not what I wanted.
It'll have to be done again.

Answer these questions:

What does he think of the latest design?
Why isn't it what he wanted?
What will have to happen?
How does the other man feel?

▶ Listen to this:

1st woman: Here's the dress you wanted made.
2nd woman: Oh, dear!
1st woman: What's the matter?
2nd woman: It's not what I asked for.
1st woman: What's wrong with it?
2nd woman: It's not the right material.
Or the right colour.
I can't possibly accept it.
1st woman: That *is* a pity!

▶ Now say this (listen and repeat):

Here's the one you wanted.
We've made it.
We've made the one you wanted.
It's the one you wanted made.
What's the matter?
What's wrong with it?
It's not what I asked for.
I can't possibly accept it.

Look at this:

I want	it	made.
		repaired.
I'll get		cleaned.
		replaced.

Answer these questions:

Is it the one she wanted made?
What's wrong with it?
Is she going to accept it?
What does she say?

Unit 13
Certainty and doubt

Are you sure it goes there?
Yes, positive.

I wonder if she'd like to go?
I doubt it.

Surely you're not going to wear
that hat?
I certainly am!

Do you think he'll be President?
He might.

▶ Listen to this:

>*Man:* Does this bus go to Hammersmith?
>*Woman:* Yes, I think so.
>It's a number eleven.
>That goes to Hammersmith.
>*Man:* Are you sure?
>*Woman:* Yes, positive.
>Look – it says 'Hammersmith' on the front.

▶ Now say this (listen and repeat):

>Does it go there?
>Yes, I think so.
>Are you sure?
>Yes, positive.

▶ Listen to this:

>*Woman:* Does the 12 go to Westminster?
>*Man:* I'm not sure.
>*Woman:* Which bus does go there?
>*Man:* I couldn't say.

Answer these questions:

>Which bus goes to Hammersmith?
>Are you sure?
>Does the 12 go there, too?
>Does the 11 go to Westminster?
>Does the 12?

▶ Listen to this:

>*Woman:* Look! A jazz concert.
>I wonder if your mother would like to go?
>*Man:* I doubt it.
>*Woman:* Why not?
>*Man:* It'll be too noisy.
>*Woman:* I thought she liked jazz.
>*Man:* Well, she certainly doesn't like loud jazz.
>And that concert will definitely be loud.

▶ Now say this (listen and repeat):

>I wonder if she'd like it.
>I doubt it.
>I wonder if it goes there.
>I think so, but I'm not sure.

Are you sure she'll like it?
Yes, positive.

Look at this:

Does it go there?	I think so —	yes, I'm sure it does.
I wonder if it goes there?		but I'm not sure.

Will she	like it?	Yes, I'm sure she will.
I wonder if she'll		I doubt it.

Answer these questions:

Does his mother like jazz?
Will she like this concert?
Why not?

▶ Listen to this:

1st woman: Surely you're not going to wear that hat?
2nd woman: I certainly am.
        Why shouldn't I?
1st woman: Well — isn't it a bit daring?
2nd woman: I don't think so.
        It's very smart.
        I'm definitely going to wear it.
1st woman: Oh, well — please yourself.

▶ Now say this (listen and repeat):

Surely you're not going to wear it?
I certainly am.
Surely you're not going to tell him?
I certainly am.
I'm definitely going to tell him.
I'm definitely going to wear it.
Why shouldn't I?

▶ Listen to this:

1st man: Do you think he'll be the next President?
2nd man: He might.
        But I doubt it.

Look at this:

EXPRESSING CERTAINTY	EXPRESSING DOUBT
I'm sure it does.	Are you sure?
I'm sure it will.	I'm not sure.
I'm positive.	I don't think so.
Definitely.	Surely you're not going to . . . ?
I certainly am.	I wonder if . . . ?
I'm definitely going to.	He might . . . but I doubt it.
Yes, I'm certain.	I couldn't say.

Now ask your friends questions like this:

Are you going to . . . ?
Do you think he will . . . ?
Does it go there . . . ?
Are you sure it does . . . ?
Do you think she'll like . . . ?
Surely you're not going to . . . ?

Make up some questions to which the answer could be:

He might . . .
She might . . .
It might . . .   } but I doubt it.
They might . . .

Unit 14
Advice

You should take some exercise.

You shouldn't eat too much.

I wouldn't buy it if I were you.

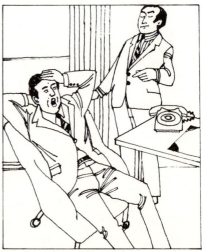

Why don't you go to bed earlier?

Read this. It is some good advice about how to live a healthy life:

You should get plenty of sleep.
You should eat food which is good for you.
You should take some exercise every day.

You shouldn't eat too much.
You shouldn't work too hard.
You shouldn't worry about the future.

Now read this:

You OUGHT TO get some exercise.
You OUGHT NOT TO work too hard.

Look at this:

You	should ought to	get plenty of sleep. take some exercise.

You	shouldn't ought not to oughtn't to	work too hard.

Now give your friend some advice:

. . . . sleep . . . .
. . . . eat . . . .
. . . . exercise
. . . . work . . . .
. . . . worry . . . .

Can you give your friend some advice about these things?

read	get up late
drive	play your radio
wash	leave your money
clean your teeth	swim
clean your shoes	cross the street
park your car	smoke

▶ Listen to this:

> *1st woman:* Look at this lovely scarf!
> I *must* get it.
> *2nd woman:* I wouldn't buy it if I were you.
> *1st woman:* Why not?
> It's just the colour I want.
> *2nd woman:* Yes, the colour's all right.
> But it's not very good quality.
> I'd try somewhere else if I were you.
> *1st woman:* Perhaps you're right.

▶ Now say this (listen and repeat):

> I wouldn't buy it if I were you.
> I would try somewhere else if I were you.
> I'd try somewhere else if I were you.

Look at this:

I	would 'd	try somewhere else	if I were you.

Now give your friend some advice about these things:

> Look at that super house! I'd love to live there.
> I'd really like to see that film.
> Let's try this restaurant.
> I'm going to Greece by train.
> That's a beautiful chair! I think I'll buy it.
> I'll walk home on my own.
> I don't think I'll take an umbrella.
> I don't think I'll change any money.
> Here's a parking space!
> I think I'll have another piece of chocolate cake.

Here are some ideas for your answers:

get fat	take too long
not very good	dangerous
too expensive	need some
too noisy	need one
too far from the shops	prohibited/not allowed

▶ Listen to this:

> *Man:* I'm always getting lost in this town.
> *Woman:* Why don't you buy a street map?
> *Man:* Yes, perhaps I should.

> *1st woman:* I can't get into this dress any more!
> *2nd woman:* Why don't you go on a diet?
> *1st woman:* Yes, perhaps I should.

> *1st man:* I always feel tired in the mornings.
> *2nd man:* Why don't you go to bed earlier?
> *1st man:* Yes, perhaps I should.

▶ Now YOU give the advice. Listen, and then speak:

> I'm always getting lost in this town.
> I can't get into this dress any more.
> I always feel tired in the mornings.

Answer your friend when he gives you advice.
Listen, and then speak:

> Why don't you buy a street map?
> . . . .
> Why don't you go on a diet?
> . . . .
> Why don't you go to bed earlier?
> . . . .

Look at this:

You should You ought to Why don't you	go to bed earlier.

Unit 15
Assumption

They'll be sitting on deck —
and *they'll* be taking some exercise.

It must be at least 100 years old.

Do you think he's coming?
No, he must have forgotten.

The bus must have gone.
It *can't* have!

▶ Listen to this:

>   *1st woman:* The cruise has started.
>   What do you think David and Barbara are doing now?
>   *2nd woman:* They'll be sitting on deck enjoying the sunshine.
>   *1st woman:* And what about Helen and Mike?
>   *2nd Woman:* Oh, they'll be taking some exercise.

▶ Now say this (listen and repeat):

>   I'm not sure what they're doing.
>   But I can imagine what they are doing.
>   They'll be sitting on deck.
>   They'll be enjoying the sunshine.
>   The others will be taking some exercise.

Look at this:

I think they are doing it now.	→	They'll be doing it now.

Answer these questions:

>   What do you think David and Barbara are doing?
>   What do you think Helen and Mike are doing?
>   What do you imagine the President of the United States
>   is doing now?
>   What do you imagine the Queen is doing now?

▶ Listen to this:

>   *Woman:* That house looks interesting.
>   *Man:* Yes, it must be at least 100 years old.

>   *1st woman:* I can't open the door.
>   *2nd woman:* It must be locked.

>   *1st man:* I can't find my newspaper.
>   *2nd man:* You must be sitting on it.

>   *Woman:* What was that noise?
>   *Man:* It was the pilot putting the wheels down.
>   We must be coming in to land.
>   Are you frightened?
>   *Woman:* Frightened? You must be joking!

▶• Now say this (listen and repeat):

> It must be very old.
> It must be locked.
> You must be sitting on it.
> We must be coming in to land.
> You must be joking!

Look at this:

		old. locked.
It	must be	
You		sitting on it. joking.

Now you respond in the same way:

> That house looks interesting.
> . . . .
> I can't open the door.
> . . . .
> I can't find my newspaper.
> . . . .
> Are you frightened?
> . . . .

▶ Listen to this:

> *Woman:* John's very late.
> Do you think he's coming?
> *Man:* Well, it doesn't seem like it.
> He must have forgotten.
> *Woman:* I suppose you're right.
> He can't have remembered.

Look at this:

He MUST HAVE forgotten. They MUST HAVE drunk it all.	=	He CAN'T HAVE remembered. They CAN'T HAVE left us any.

▶ Listen to this:

> *Woman:* What's happened to the bus?
> *Man:* It must have gone.
> *Woman:* It *can't* have!
> It's not time yet.

▶ Now say this (listen and repeat):

> He must have forgotten.
> He can't have remembered.
> They can't have left us any.
> They must have drunk it all.
> The bus must have gone.
> It *can't* have – it's not time yet!

Look at these ways of stating assumptions:

> They'll be doing it now.
> It must be old. (It can't be new.)
> You must be joking. (You can't be serious.)
> You must be sitting on it.
> He must have done it.
> She can't have done it.

Now answer these questions. Use the words given to make an assumption in your reply:

1.	Why is he shouting?	(angry)
2.	Why is she running?	(late for work)
3.	Why is he still in bed?	(ill)
4.	Why is the baby crying?	(hungry)
5.	Why do you think he's standing there?	(waiting for . . .)
6.	What's that funny smell?	(cakes . . . burning)
7.	What's that noise?	(raining)
8.	Why isn't the secretary here?	(having lunch)
9.	What has he done with his old car?	(sold)
10.	Why didn't the bus stop?	(full)
11.	Why has the light gone out?	(switched)
12.	Why did it break so easily?	(very old)
13.	Why hasn't he answered my letter?	(received it)
14.	Why hasn't he given our homework back?	(corrected it)
15.	Why does he look so cheerful?	(heard the bad news)

Unit 16
Annoyance and reproach

What do you think you're doing?

What do you mean by smoking my cigars?

Why on earth didn't you wake me?

You might have left me some coffee!

▶ Listen to this:

> *Woman:* What do you think you're doing?
> *Man:* I'm just getting myself some milk.
> *Woman:* How dare you!
> You've no right to help yourself.
> I'll have none left for the morning.
> *Man:* I'm sorry.
> I didn't think you'd mind.

▶ Now say this (listen and repeat):

> What do you think you're doing?
> How dare you?
> You've no right to do that!
> I'm sorry.
> I didn't think you'd mind.

▶ Listen to this:

> *1st man:* What do you mean by smoking my best cigars?
> *2nd man:* Oh, I'm sorry.
> I didn't think you'd mind.
> *1st man:* You might have asked!

▶ Now say this (listen and repeat):

> What do you mean by helping yourself?
> What do you mean by taking my milk?
> What do you mean by smoking my cigars?
> You might have asked!
> You could have asked!

Look at this:

What do you	think you're doing? mean by doing that?

You	might could	have asked!

Now practise saying:

> 'What do you mean by . . . ing?'

Your neighbour will reply by saying:

'Sorry. I didn't think you'd mind.' —

sitting in my chair	drinking all the coffee
playing my records	parking here
using my phone	coming home so late
wearing those clothes	inviting your friends in

▶ Listen to this:

> *Man:* Look at the time!
> I'll be late!
> Why on earth didn't you wake me?
> *Woman:* I didn't know you were going out.
> Why on earth didn't you wind the clock?
> *Man:* You could have reminded me!

▶ Now say this (listen and repeat):

Why on earth didn't you come in?
Why on earth didn't you wake me?
Why on earth didn't you wind the clock?
Why on earth didn't you remind me?
You could have reminded me!

Now practise saying 'Why on earth didn't you . . . ?'

come earlier	buy some
tell me	ask me
phone him	help her
bring some money	wake him

▶ Listen to this:

> *Man:* Is there any coffee left?
> *Woman:* I don't think there is.
> *Man:* You might have left me some!
> *Woman:* Sorry. We didn't think.

> *Woman:* What time does the meeting start?
> *Man:* Oh — there's no meeting this evening.
> It's been cancelled.
> *Woman:* Somebody might have told me!
> *Man:* Sorry. We forgot.

▶ Now say this (listen and repeat):

You might have left me some!
Somebody might have told me!

You might have phoned me!
They might have waited!
You might have left a message!

Look at these ways of expressing annoyance or reproach:

What do you think you're doing?
How dare you!
You've no right to do that!
What do you mean by smoking my cigars?
You might have asked!
Somebody could have told me!
Why on earth didn't you tell me?

Now make sentences to practise.
First, make sentences beginning:

'How dare you (. . . do that)!'

Then, make sentences beginning:

'You've no right to . . . !'

Then, make sentences beginning:

'What do you mean by . . .ing . . . ?'

Use this list, then add further examples of your own:

smoke my cigars
borrow my books without permission
sit in my chair
use all the hot water
make long-distance phone calls
put your dirty shoes on my sofa

Unit 17
Enthusiasm and pleasure

We're having a marvellous time.
The weather has been gorgeous.
It's a fantastic place.

How lovely to see you!
You look awfully well!
You haven't changed a bit!

The play was excellent.
The acting was superb.
The sets were terrific.

Read this letter:

Dear Mother,
We're having a marvellous time here; the villa is in a delightful setting, and the views are superb. The housekeeper is extremely helpful, and prepares meals which are absolutely delicious. There are some fascinating villages near by, and one or two magnificent churches. The weather has been gorgeous, and we've had some splendid bathing. There's a charming little night-club not far away, and the musicians play terrific jazz. You *must* come here one day, it's a fantastic place.

With love from
Susan

▶ Listen to this:

What sort of time are you having? — Marvellous!
What's the setting of the villa like? — Delightful!
What are the views like? — Superb!
What's the housekeeper like? — Extremely helpful!
What are the meals like? — Absolutely delicious!
What are the villages like? — Fascinating!
What are the local churches like? — Magnificent!
What's the weather like? — Gorgeous!
What's the bathing been like? — Splendid!
What's the night-club like? — Charming!
How would you describe the place? — Fantastic!

Now practise these questions and answers with your neighbour:

time?	local churches?
setting of the villa?	weather?
views?	bathing?
housekeeper?	night-club?
meals?	music?
villages?	place?

▶ Listen to this:

1st woman: Mary!
2nd woman: Susan! How lovely to see you after all this time!
1st woman: Yes, it's been ages, hasn't it?
You look awfully well!
2nd woman: So do you!
You haven't changed a bit!
That's a super dress you're wearing.
1st woman: I'm glad you like it; I got it in a charming little boutique near here.

2nd woman: Are you still working?
1st woman: Yes, I've got a marvellous job. How about you?
2nd woman: No — actually, I'm going to have a baby.
1st woman: Oh, that's wonderful news!

▶ Now say this (listen and repeat):

It's good to see you.
You look awfully well.
You haven't changed a bit.
That's a super dress you're wearing.
I've got a marvellous job.
That's wonderful news.

Answer these questions:

Have they seen each other recently?
How long is it since they saw each other?
How does the second woman look?
What's the first woman's dress like?
Where did she get it?
Does the first woman like her job?
What's the wonderful news?

▶ Listen to this:

Woman: Did you go to the theatre last night?
Man: Yes, I did.
Woman: What did you think of the play?
Man: It was excellent.
I really enjoyed it.
It was a thrilling plot,
the acting was superb,
and the sets were terrific.
It's an outstanding play.
A marvellous evening's entertainment.

Answer these questions:

What did he think of the play?
What did he think of the plot?
What was the acting like?
What were the sets like?
Did he enjoy the evening?

Look at all these words which have been used to express enthusiasm and pleasure:

marvellous	fascinating	charming
delightful	magnificent	terrific
superb	gorgeous	fantastic
delicious	splendid	super
wonderful	excellent	thrilling

What did each word describe?
What else could you describe with these words?

Unit 18
Indifference

Look! The Olympic Games!
I couldn't care less.

I thought you *liked*
spaghetti!
Not particularly.

We've missed the bus.
We might as well walk.

▶ Listen to this:

> *Man:* Shall we go out for a meal this evening?
> *Woman:* I don't really mind.
> *Man:* We could go to that new Chinese restaurant.
> *Woman:* I suppose we could.
> *Man:* Come on! Let's try it.
> *Woman:* All right, if you really want to.

> *Woman:* Look! It's the start of the Olympic Games!
> *Man:* So what?
> *Woman:* You want to watch, don't you?
> *Man:* Not really.
> I couldn't care less about the Olympic Games.
> *Woman:* Please yourself!

▶ Now say this (listen and repeat):

> I don't really mind.
> I suppose we could.
> All right, if you really want to.
> So what?
> I couldn't care less.
> Please yourself!

▶ Now you answer in the same way:

> Shall we go to the cinema?
>
> . . . .
> We could go and see that new James Bond film.
>
> . . . .
> Come on! Let's go.
>
> . . . .
> There's some modern jazz on the radio!
>
> . . . .
> You'd like to listen, wouldn't you?
>
> . . . .
> . . . .

Look at this:

Shall we . . . ?	→	I don't really mind.
We could . . .	→	I suppose we could.
Come on, let's . . .	→	All right, if you really want to.
Look! It's . . .	→	So what?
You want to, don't you?	→	Not really. I couldn't care less.

▶ Listen to this:

> *Woman:* Shall I cook some spaghetti?
> *Man:* If you like.
> *Woman:* You don't sound very keen.
> I thought you *liked* spaghetti.
> *Man:* Not particularly.
> I'm not very fond of Italian food.

▶ Now say this (listen and repeat):

I'm not very fond of spaghetti.
I'm not very keen on spaghetti.
She's not very fond of football.
She's not very keen on football.
She couldn't care less about football.
I couldn't care less about modern jazz.
I thought you *liked* jazz.
Not particularly.

Look at this:

Would you like some rice pudding?	No thanks. I'm not very keen on rice pudding.

Now practise asking and answering in the same way:

cold milk	fish and chips
bacon and eggs	cornflakes
spaghetti	lager
toast	marmalade
mustard	chocolate

Look at this:

Would you like to go to the cinema?	Not really. I'm not very fond of the cinema.

Now practise asking and answering in the same way:

a football match	a pop festival
a jazz concert	a Chinese restaurant
a horse race	a political meeting
a boxing match	the opera
the swimming-pool	the shops

Be careful in your answers! Use these words instead of the words in the questions:

football   pop music
jazz   Chinese food
horse-racing   political speeches
boxing   opera
swimming   shopping

▶ Listen to this:

    Woman: Shall we walk home?
      Man: If you insist . . .
    Woman: Well, we've just missed a bus,
            and it's a long time till the next one.
      Man: Oh, well. In that case I suppose we might as well walk.
    Woman: Yes, we might as well.

▶ Now say this (listen and repeat):

We might as well walk.
We might as well stay in.
We might as well wait.
We might as well come back tomorrow.
We might as well take a taxi.

Unit 19
Sympathy and encouragement

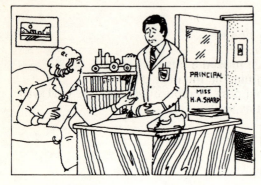

I'm afraid you haven't passed.
I'm terribly sorry.
You can always take it again.

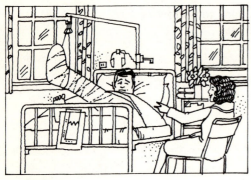

Cheer up!
It could have been a lot worse.

It can't be helped.
It's not the end of the world!

▶ Listen to this:

> *Woman:* I've just got the examination results.
> I'm afraid you haven't passed.
> *Man:* Oh, no!
> I can't have failed — surely?
> *Woman:* I'm afraid so.
> I'm terribly sorry.
> *Man:* Whatever am I going to tell my parents?
> *Woman:* Don't worry about that.
> I'm sure they'll understand.
> After all, it was a very difficult exam.
> *Man:* What am I to do?
> *Woman:* You can always take it again.

▶ Now say this (listen and repeat):

> I'm afraid you haven't passed.
> I'm terribly sorry.
> Don't worry about it.
> I'm sure they'll understand.
> You can always take it again.

▶ Listen to this:

> *Woman:* What a shame about your accident.
> What a way to end your holiday!
> *Man:* Yes, it was bad luck.
> I suppose I should have been more careful.
> And I feel so helpless lying here. And so *miserable*!
> *Woman:* Oh, come on!
> Cheer up!
> It could have been a lot worse, you know.
> I'm sure you'll be out of here in no time.
> *Man:* I'm not so sure.
> They say it'll be a long job.
> I can't see myself doing any sport for several months.
> It's very depressing.
> *Woman:* Never mind.
> Look on the bright side.
> You'll be back in the team next season,
> you'll see!

▶ Now say this (listen and repeat):

What a shame!
Come on!
Cheer up!
It could have been worse.
Never mind.
Look on the bright side.
You'll be out in no time.
You'll see!

Look at the first picture, and answer these questions:

Has he passed his exam?
What has he done?
Is he surprised?
How do you think he feels?
What is he most worried about?
Is the Principal angry with him?
What does she say to encourage him?
Have you ever failed an exam?

Now look at the second picture, and answer these questions:

What has happened to the man?
What exactly has he done?
How do you think he did it?
Where is he now?
How does he feel about being there?
What depresses him most?
How does the woman try to encourage him?
Have you ever been in hospital?

▶ Listen to this:

     Man: Just look what I've done!
          It was a new car.
          Whatever am I going to do?
Woman: Look — it's happened;
          and it can't be helped.
          It's not the end of the world, you know.
          And you had a lucky escape.
     Man: Yes, I know.
          I'm all right.
          It's the *car* . . . !
Woman: Well, they can do marvellous repairs, you know.
          When they've finished it'll look just like new.
     Man: I hope you're right.

Woman: Of course I am.
Cheer up!

▶ Now say this (listen and repeat):

It's happened, and it can't be helped.
It's not the end of the world, you know.
You had a lucky escape.
They can do marvellous repairs, you know.
Cheer up!

Look at these ways of encouraging someone:

What a shame!   It can't be helped.
Never mind.   You'll soon be out.
Don't worry about it.   It could have been worse.
You can always . . .   Cheer up!
Look on the bright side!

What would you say to get these people to cheer up?

a friend who has failed the driving test;
a mother whose young son has gone into hospital;
a friend who has missed getting a good job;
a writer who has had a book refused by a publisher.

Unit 20
Disappointment and disgust

I don't think much of it, I can tell you.

What a mess!
Yes, it's disgraceful.

Just look!
It's disgusting!

Oh, no!
Isn't it awful?

Read this letter:

> Dear Mum and Dad,
> I arrived safely after a good journey, and the town looks quite interesting. The people I'm staying with seem very nice, but I must say I'm disappointed in my room. It's terribly small, and not very well furnished. The bed is narrow, hard and lumpy, and the room is dark, as there's only one small window, and no view. There's nowhere for me to study: just a chair, but no table. I haven't got a wardrobe, just a small chest of drawers, so I shall have to keep some of my clothes in my trunk. I don't think much of it, I can tell you, and I was pretty depressed when I saw it. It's only for four weeks, though, so I suppose I'll just have to put up with it.

▶ Now say this (listen and repeat):

> I must say I'm disappointed in it.
> I don't think much of it.
> I was pretty depressed when I saw it.
> I suppose I'll just have to put up with it.

Answer these questions:

> What does he think of the town?
> What does he think of the people he's staying with?
> What's wrong with his room?
> What's wrong with the bed?
> Why is the room dark?
> What's the view like?
> What hasn't he got in the room?
> What has he got?
> How did he feel when he first saw it?
> What does he suppose he'll have to do?

▶ Listen to this:

> *Woman:* What a mess!
>   Just look at all this litter!
>   *Man:* Yes, it's disgraceful.
>   I don't know what people are thinking of,
>   to leave it like this.
> *Woman:* They ought to be ashamed of themselves.
>   It ought not to be allowed.
>   They should be made to clear it up.
>   *Man:* I agree.

▶ Now say this (listen and repeat):

> What a mess!
> It's disgraceful!
> They ought to be ashamed of themselves!
> It ought not to be allowed!
> They should be made to clear it up!

▶ Listen to this:

> *Man:* Just look at those two!
> What a way to dress!
> I think it's disgusting!
> *Woman:* I must admit they look pretty untidy.
> I suppose they feel more comfortable
> dressed like that.
> People should please themselves, surely?
> *Man:* I'm not so sure about that.
> They don't have to look at themselves.
> It's offensive to other people.

Now answer these questions:

> What do you think of the way the young people are dressed?
> Do you agree with the man or the woman?
> Do you think people should always please themselves how they dress?
> Does the way people dress tell you something about them?
> Why do you think these two are dressed like this?

Look at these ways of expressing disgust:

> What a . . . !
> It's disgraceful/disgusting/offensive.
> It ought not to be allowed.
> What are they thinking of?

What things do you find offensive?

> litter?
> noise?
> other people's behaviour?
> television advertising?
> anything else?

▶ Listen to this:

> *Woman:* Oh, no!
> Look at the view from the window!
> *Man:* Oh, dear.
> That's dreadful.
> Not at all what I expected.
> *Woman:* They promised us a sea view.
> *Man:* Well . . . you *can* just see the sea –
> between the factory chimneys.
> *Woman:* Isn't it awful?
> I can't bear to look at it.
> I don't think I can stand this place for two weeks.
> *Man:* Well, it can't be helped.
> We'll just have to put up with it.

▶ Now say this (listen and repeat):

> Oh, no!
> How dreadful.
> Isn't it awful?
> I can't bear to look at it.
> I don't think I can stand it.

Unit 21
Commands

Get your books out.
Turn to page 47.

Stand still!
Don't move, or I'll fire.

Get out of my house and don't
come back!

Sell the product!
Increase your sales!

▶ Listen to this teacher talking to his class:

Sit down.
Stop talking.
Be quiet, I said!
Get your books out.
Turn to page 47.
Do exercise 3.
Don't draw the map, just write the answers.
You are to stay here till I get back.
You are not to talk to one another.

▶ Now say this (listen and repeat):

He told them to sit down and to stop talking.
He told them to get their books out,
and to turn to page 47.
He told them to do exercise 3,
but not to draw the map.
He told them to stay there till he got back,
and not to talk to one another.

Look at this:

Do You are to do	this.

Don't do You are not to do	that.

Do	this	and but	don't do	that.

▶ Listen to this frontier guard shouting commands to a person trying to cross the frontier illegally:

Stand still!
Stay where you are!
Hands up!
Don't move, or I'll fire.

Now . . . put your hands on your head . . .
and come over here, . . . slowly.

▶ Now say this (listen and repeat):

He told me to stand still and
stay where I was.
He told me to put my hands up.
He told me not to move, or he'd fire.

Look at this:

'Stay where you are!'	→	He told me to stay where I was.
'Don't move!'	→	He told me not to move.
'Stop talking!'	→	He told them to stop talking.

▶ Listen to this angry father speaking to his daughter's boy-friend:

Go away!
Leave my daughter alone!
Get out of my house and don't come back!
Don't try to contact her.
Find someone else.

▶ Now say this (listen and repeat):

He told him to go away and to leave his daughter alone.
He told him to get out of the house and not to come back.
He told him not to try to contact her.
He told him to find someone else.

▶ Listen to the sales manager speaking to an unsatisfactory salesman:

Go out.
Find new customers.
Sell the product.
Increase your sales.
Don't come back until you have succeeded.

▶ Now say this (listen and repeat):

He told him to go out and find new customers.
He told him to sell the product and increase his sales.
He told him not to come back until he had succeeded.

Look at this:

'Don't come back until you HAVE succeeded.'	→	He told him not to come back until he HAD succeeded.
'Don't phone me until you HAVE found one.'	→	She told him not to phone her until he HAD found one.

Say what you think the speaker's actual words were:

> He told her to phone him at his hotel every evening.
> She told him to clear up the mess he had made.
> The policeman told him not to park there.
> The director told the manager to improve the sales figures and not to ask for any more staff until he had done so.
> She told him not to use the car without her permission.
> The teacher told them to stand still and not to talk.

What would you say if:

> you wanted someone to go away and not to come back?
> you wanted your secretary to type something again and bring it to you as soon as she had finished it?
> you wanted someone not to touch something?

Unit 22
Requests

Could you just hold this for me?

Would you mind waiting?

I wonder if I could trouble you to change a £5 note?

Would you be so kind as to lay the table?

▶ Listen to this:

>*Man:* Could you just hold this for me?
>*Woman:* What are you doing?
>Is something wrong?
>*Man:* Yes, but I've nearly fixed it.
>Just take it, will you?
>*Woman:* Oh, yes, of course.
>I'm sorry − I wasn't thinking.

▶ Now say this (listen and repeat):

>Could you hold this for me?
>Could you just help me?
>Could you just take this?
>Just hold it for me, will you?
>Just help me, will you?
>Just take it, will you?
>Yes, of course.

Look at this:

Could you	JUST	hold this for me?
	JUST	take it, will you?

▶ Listen to this:

>*Man:* Good morning; my name's Gray.
>I have an appointment with Mr Campbell at eleven o'clock.
>*Woman:* Yes . . . Will you take a seat, please?
>I'll tell Mr Campbell you're here.

>*   *   *   *   *

>Mr Gray, Mr Campbell has someone with him at present.
>He should be free soon.
>Would you mind waiting?
>*Man:* Not at all.

▶ Now say this (listen and repeat):

>Will you take a seat, Mr Gray?
>Will you sit here, please?
>Would you just wait a moment?
>Yes, of course.

Would you mind waiting?
Not at all.

Look at this:

COULD WILL WOULD	you	HOLD it for me? WAIT a moment? HELP me?

Yes, of course.

WOULD you MIND	HOLDING it for me? WAITING a moment? HELPING me?

Not at all.

Now respond to these requests in the same way:

Will you come this way, please?
Would you just take a seat?
Would you mind coming back in half an hour?
Could you just take it upstairs for me?
Would you mind parking somewhere else?
Will you fill in this form, please?
Would you mind filling in this form?
Would you just fill in this form?

▶ Listen to this:

Man: Can I help you?
Woman: Yes . . .
I wonder if I could trouble you to change
a five pound note?
Man: I'll see.
What would you like: five ones?
Woman: Yes, please, that would be fine.
Man: Here you are.
Woman: Thank you. I'm most grateful.

▶ Now say this (listen and repeat):

> I wonder if I could trouble you to change this?
> I wonder if I could trouble you to move your car?
> I wonder if I could trouble you to explain this?
> Thank you. I'm most grateful.

▶ Listen to this:

> *Woman:* Thomas, would you be so kind as to lay the table for me?
> I'm busy in the kitchen.
> *Man:* Of course! Where are the things?
> *Woman:* They're all here.
> *Man:* Right! I'll do it straight away.
> *Woman:* Thanks a lot.
> I'm most grateful.

▶ Now say this (listen and repeat):

> Would you be so kind as to lay the table?
> Would you be so kind as to do it for me?
> Would you be so kind as to close the window?
> Would you be so kind as to call my sister?
> Of course! I'll do it straight away.

Look at this:

Could you Will you Would you I wonder if I could trouble you to Would you be so kind as to	DO it for me?

Yes, of course.

Would you MIND DOING it for me?

Not at all.

Now practise making requests, using all these forms:

wait a moment	tell him I'm here	open the window
take a seat	change £5 for me	clean these shoes
hold this for me	come this way	lay the table
help me	phone my aunt	explain this

Unit 23
Wishes

I wish I had time to clean it!
Shall I do it?
I wish you would.

If only I had more money . . . !

I'd like these filed.

I'd rather you stayed here and wrote the postcards.

▶ Listen to this:

> *Man:* I wish I had time to clean the car.
> It's filthy.
> *Woman:* Shall I do it for you?
> I've got time, and I wouldn't mind.
> *Man:* Oh, I wish you would.
>
> *Woman:* I wish I knew the times of the trains to London.
> I can't phone, as our phone's out of order.
> *Man:* If you like, I'll pop down to the station and find out.
> *Woman:* Oh, I wish you would.

▶ Now say this (listen and repeat):

> I wish I had time to do it.
> I wish I knew the answer.
> I wish I had time.
> I wish I knew.
> Oh, I wish you would.

Look at this:

I wish I	HAD	time.
	KNEW	his name.
	LIVED	somewhere else.
	COULD	play the piano.
	LOOKED	younger.

I wish	you	WOULD	do it for me.
	he	WOULD	go away.
	she	LIVED	nearer.
	we	HAD	more money.
	they	WOULD BE	quiet.

Can you see the difference between:

I wish he WENT home at the same time as I do.

and

I wish he WOULD GO home!

and between:

I wish I DROVE a Mercedes.

and

I wish he WOULD DRIVE more carefully.

Look:

> I wish he WENT   (but he doesn't . . .)
> I wish I DROVE   (but I don't . . .)
> I wish he WOULD DRIVE
> I wish he WOULD GO   (and perhaps he will!)

▶ Listen to this:

> *Woman:* If only I had more money,
>   I could fly to Canada and see them.
>   *Man:* Perhaps your bank manager will let you have a loan.
> *Woman:* Oh, if only he would!

▶ Now say this (listen and repeat):

> I wish I had more money.
> If only I had more money I could do it.
> If only I had more money . . . !
> I wish he would let me have a loan.
> If only he would!

Now express your wishes, beginning with:

> I wish I . . .
> I wish he would . . .
> If only I . . .
> If only he would . . .

▶ Listen to this:

> *Woman:* What would you like done while you're away?
>   *Man:* Well . . .
>   I'd like this typed.
>   I'd like these corrections made.
>   I'd like this copied.
>   I'd like these letters filed.
> *Woman:* Does anything else need doing?
>   *Man:* Well, the office needs tidying up.
>   It really needs redecorating.
>   I don't suppose you could get that done?
> *Woman:* There's not much time.
>   But I'll see if it can be done.
>   *Man:* I'd be glad if you would.

▶ Now say this (listen and repeat):

This needs doing.
I'd like it done.
This needs typing.
I'd like it typed.
These need filing.
I'd like them filed.
The office needs redecorating.
I'd like it redecorated.

Look at this:

	IT	needs DOING.
I'd like	IT	DONE.

and this:

I WISH I'd BE GLAD IF	you would.

Now say what needs doing, and what you'd like done:

cleaning	— cleaned	feeding	— fed
repairing	— repaired	washing	— washed
painting	— painted	checking	— checked
replacing	— replaced	anything else?	

▶ Listen to this:

Man: Would you like me to come with you?
Woman: I'd rather you stayed here and looked after the things.
Man: Do you want to write the postcards?
Woman: I'd rather you wrote them.

▶ Now say this (listen and repeat):

I'd rather you stayed here.
I'd rather you wrote them.
I'd rather you told him.
I'd rather you did it.
I'd rather you cooked them.

Practise making suggestions to each other, and replying with 'I'd rather you . . .'

Unit 24
Obligation

She usually has to stand in the train.

We must help him — he's obviously in trouble.

You mustn't light that cigarette!

I've made ten copies.
You needn't have made so many!

▶ Listen to this:

These are some things I have to do when I go to work . . .
I have to get up at seven.
I have to leave home at eight.
I have to be in the office by nine.
I have to type all day.
I have to do my shopping in the lunch-hour.
I usually have to stand in the train in the evening.
I have to cook a meal when I get home.

▶ Now say this (listen and repeat):

She has to get up at seven.
She has to leave home at eight.
She has to be in the office by nine.
She has to type all day.
She has to do her shopping in the lunch-hour.
She usually has to stand in the train in the evening.
She has to cook a meal when she gets home.

Answer these questions:

What time does she have to leave home in the morning?
Why do you think she has to do her shopping in the lunch-hour?
Why do you think she has to stand in the train in the evening?
What does she have to do when she gets home?
What time do you have to get up in the morning?

▶ Listen to this:

Man: I must phone my wife — she'll be worried about me.
Woman: We must help him — he's obviously in trouble.

Look at this:

I HAVE TO do it . . . because circumstances make it necessary.
I MUST do it . . . because my conscience tells me it is necessary.

▶ Listen to this:

Woman: Do we have to work on Saturdays?
Man: No, you don't.

Man: Shall I wait for you?
Woman: No, you needn't.

▶ Now say this (listen and repeat):

> She doesn't have to work on Saturdays.
> She says he needn't wait for her.

Look at this:

You DON'T HAVE TO . . .	as a general rule.
You NEEDN'T . . .	in this particular case.

▶ Listen to this:

> *Woman:* You mustn't light that cigarette!
> *Man:* Why not?
> *Woman:* You're not allowed to smoke in here.

Now say this (listen and repeat):

> You mustn't do it.
> You're not allowed to do it.
> It's not allowed.
> You mustn't smoke where it's not allowed.

▶ Listen to this:

> *Woman:* I had to wait ages for a bus this morning. Did you?
> *Man:* No, I was lucky.
>   I didn't have to wait at all.
>   A bus came just as I got to the stop.

> *Woman:* I've made ten copies.
> *Man:* You needn't have made so many.
>   Two would have been enough.

Look at this:

I DIDN'T HAVE TO DO IT . . .	I didn't do it because it wasn't necessary.
I NEEDN'T HAVE DONE IT . . .	I did it, although it wasn't necessary.

▶ Now say this (listen and repeat):

> She had to wait ages for the bus.
> He didn't have to wait at all.
> She's made ten copies.
> She needn't have made so many.

Look at this:

Obligation	No obligation	Negative obligation or prohibition
'It is necessary' ↓	'It isn't necessary' ↓	'It is forbidden' 'It isn't allowed' ↓
I HAVE TO I MUST	You DON'T HAVE TO You NEEDN'T	You MUSTN'T You'RE NOT ALLOWED TO
'It was necessary' ↓	'It wasn't necessary' ↓	'It wasn't allowed' ↓
I HAD TO	I DIDN'T HAVE TO YOU NEEDN'T HAVE . . .	I WASN'T ALLOWED TO
'It will be necessary' ↓	'It won't be necessary' ↓	'It won't be allowed' ↓
I'LL HAVE TO	You WON'T HAVE TO	You WON'T BE ALLOWED TO

Answer these questions:

> What do you have to do every day?
> What do you have to take with you when you travel to another country?
> What don't you have to do on Sundays?
> What must we do if we see someone who needs our help?
> What must we do if we want to pass our examination?
> What mustn't you do in an aeroplane when it's taking off or landing?
> What will you have to do tomorrow?
> What weren't you allowed to do when you were very young?
> Have you ever done anything that wasn't really necessary? Tell me!
> Shall I explain Unit 24 again?

Unit 25
Restraining

You shouldn't really be walking on the lawn.

Don't keep talking!
Don't keep fidgeting!
Sit still!

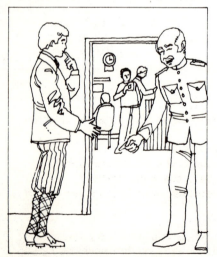

You're not supposed to wear golf-shoes in the club house.

We're thinking of cutting it down.
I'd rather you didn't.

▶ Listen to this:

> *Man:* Excuse me –
> you shouldn't really be walking on the lawn.
> *Woman:* Why not?
> *Man:* It's a private lawn, reserved for members of the college.
> *Woman:* Oh, is it?
> I didn't know.
> Thanks for telling me.

> *Woman:* You shouldn't really bring me to such expensive
> restaurants, you know.
> It's very extravagant.
> We'll never save enough money to get married!
> *Man:* Well – a little extravagance now and again doesn't do
> any harm.
> I like taking you to nice places.
> *Woman:* I enjoy it, of course.
> But you shouldn't really do it so often.

▶ Now say this (listen and repeat):

> You shouldn't really be walking on the lawn.
> You shouldn't really be doing that.
> You shouldn't really take me out so often.
> You shouldn't really do it, you know.
> You shouldn't really spend so much money.

Look at this:

You shouldn't	be doing it. do it.

and look at these two sentences:

> You shouldn't really BE SMOKING in here.
> You shouldn't really SMOKE so much.

Now make sentences like those – two sentences for each verb given:

> drive
> watch television
> eat chocolate cake
> play football
> use a dictionary

▶ Listen to this:

>   *Woman:* Don't keep talking.
>   Be quiet, and listen!
>   And don't keep fidgeting.
>   Sit still!
>
>   *Man:* Mary, will you come out with me this evening?
>   *Woman:* No! I've said no, and I mean no.
>   Don't keep asking me!

▶ Now say this (listen and repeat):

> Don't keep talking!
> Don't keep fidgeting!
> Don't keep doing that!
> Don't keep saying that!
> Don't keep asking me!

Now make sentences like those, using these words:

whisper	borrow my books
interrupt	come in and out
eat my chocolates	ask questions
smoke my cigarettes	make that noise
touch them	annoy her

▶ Listen to this:

>   *1st man:* Excuse me, sir.
>   *2nd man:* Yes, what is it?
>   *1st man:* Your shoes.
>   You're not supposed to wear golf shoes in the club-
>   house.
>   *2nd man:* Oh, of course!
>   Sorry. I forgot.
>   *1st man:* Another thing, sir.
>   *2nd man:* Yes?
>   *1st man:* You're not meant to park your car in front of the main
>   entrance.
>   *2nd man:* Oh, dear!
>   It's not my day, is it?

▶ Now say this (listen and repeat):

> You're not supposed to wear them in here.
> You're not supposed to do that.
> You're not meant to park there.
> You're not meant to do that.

Look at this:

You're not	SUPPOSED MEANT	to do that.

Tell your neighbour some things he or she is NOT SUPPOSED to do or NOT MEANT to do:

> come to school late
> use a dictionary in the examination
> leave your valuables in the classroom
> take those books home
> switch on the tape-recorder

► Listen to this:

> *Man:* We're thinking of cutting this tree down.
> Would you mind?
> *Woman:* I'd rather you didn't.
> I like having it to look at.
> And it provides shade for our garden.

► Now say this (listen and repeat):

> I'd rather you didn't cut it down.
> I'd rather you didn't.
> I'd rather you didn't tell him.
> I'd rather you didn't.

Look at this:

You SHOULDN'T REALLY You're NOT SUPPOSED TO You're NOT MEANT TO I'd RATHER YOU DIDN'T	do that.

You SHOULDN'T REALLY BE DON'T KEEP	doing that.

Index

This index shows the occurrence of new vocabulary not previously presented in Book 1.
Reference is to the number of the unit.
(*) indicates an illustration.

For the incidence of structures, see the Plan of the units at the beginning of the book.